Brian Mayne

Daily Prayer for Lent and Easter

YEAR B

columba

First published in 2006 by
THE COLUMBA PRESS
55a Spruce Avenue, Stillorgan Industrial Park,
Blackrock, Co Dublin, Ireland

Designed by Bill Bolger
Origination by The Columba Press
Printed in Ireland by ColourBooks Ltd, Dublin

ISBN 1 85607 524 9

Contents

For

Valerie

Introduction

As we believe so we pray – daily prayer for Lent and Easter Year A using the structure for daily prayer in the Prayer Book was warmly received. *Believing we pray* is offered as material for personal prayer in these seasons for Year B, constructed round the Sunday Gospels of that year. Apart from the Second Sunday in Lent the Gospels in the *Revised Common Lectionary* are the same as those in *Ordo lectio missae* so there is the opportunity for people in different denominations to reflect together and pray together.

A scripture sentence sets the tone. This is followed by a prayer of penitence, drawn from various sources, some written for this book. I have again selected classical hymns suitable for each week. Psalmody is at the centre – a refrain is provided. Over the week this may be used before or after the psalm or before and after a verse or group of verses. For the main scripture reading this year I have been able to use the provision of *Revised Common Lectionary Daily Readings* which was published in late 2005 by the Consultation on Common Texts. The compilers graciously allowed me pre-publication access to this and granted permission to include these excerpts. To use these requires having a Bible at hand. Where that is not possible the Gospel passage of the week is also printed allowing for its extended use. A canticle offers a biblical response to our reading. Possible subjects are suggested for prayer and thanksgiving. Here one's own words, however faltering, are enough. This can be concluded with the Prayer Book Collect or other prayers. For the latter I have included some of the fresh prayers from the New Zealand Prayer Book and other new sources. Finally, we pray the Lord's Prayer and a short 'ending' to send us on our way.

I hope that all who use this book will find that their faith is strengthened as 'believing we pray' and so the whole period of Lent and Easter will be a time of growth.

Brian Mayne
Saint Matthew's Day 2005

Ash Wednesday and days following

Preparation

A SENTENCE OF SCRIPTURE

Return to the Lord, your God, who is gracious and merciful, slow to anger and abounding in steadfast love.

Joel 2: 13

A PRAYER OF PENITENCE

Righteous God,
in humility and repentance
we bring our failures in caring, helping and loving,
we bring the pain we have caused others,
we bring the injustice in society of which we are a part,
to the transforming power of your grace.
Grant us the courage to accept the healing you offer
and to turn again toward the sunrise of your reign,
that we may walk with you in the promise of peace
you have willed for all the children of the earth
and have made known to us in Christ Jesus. Amen.

RCL Prayers

HYMN

Sinful, sighing to be blest;
bound, and longing to be free;
weary, waiting for my rest;
God be merciful to me.

Goodness I have none to plead,
sinfulness in all I see,
I can only bring my need;
God be merciful to me.

Broken heart and downcast eyes
dare not lift themselves to thee;
yet thou canst interpret sighs:
God be merciful to me.

From this sinful heart of mine
to thy bosom I would flee:
I am not my own, but thine;
God be merciful to me.

There is One beside the throne,
and my only hope and plea
are in him, and him alone:
God be merciful to me.

He my cause will undertake,
my interpreter will be;
he's my all; and for his sake
God be merciful to me.

John S B Monsell (1811-75)

The Word of God

PSALM 51: 1-5

Turn your face from my sins ▪
and blot out all my misdeeds.

1 Have mercy on me, O God,
in your great goodness; ▪
according to the abundance of your compassion
blot out my offences.
2 Wash me thoroughly from my wickedness ▪
and cleanse me from my sin.
3 For I acknowledge my faults ▪
and my sin is ever before me.
4 Against you only have I sinned ▪
and done what is evil in your sight,

5 So that you are justified in your sentence ▪
and righteous in your judgement.

A BIBLE READING

LENT DISCIPLINE

Ash Wednesday	*Matthew 6: 1-6, 16-21*
Thursday	*1 John 1: 3-10*
Friday	*2 Timothy 4: 1-5*
Saturday	*Matthew 9: 2-13*

or

Jesus said to the crowds, 'Beware of practising your piety before others in order to be seen by them; for then you have no reward from your Father in heaven.

'So whenever you give alms, do not sound a trumpet before you, as the hypocrites do in the synagogues and in the streets, so that they may be praised by others. Truly I tell you, they have received their reward. But when you give alms, do not let your left hand know what your right hand is doing, so that your alms may be done in secret; and your Father who sees in secret will reward you.

'And whenever you pray, do not be like the hypocrites; for they love to stand and pray in the synagogues and at the street corners, so that they may be seen by others. Truly I tell you, they have received their reward. But whenever you pray, go into your room and shut the door and pray to your Father who is in secret; and your Father who sees in secret will reward you.

Matthew 6: 1-6, 16-21

SAVIOUR OF THE WORLD

1 Jesus Saviour of the world,
come to us in your mercy: ▪
we look to you to save and help us.

2 By your cross and your life laid down,
you set your people free: ▪
we look to you to save and help us.

3 When they were ready to perish
you saved your disciples: ▪
we look to you to come to our help.

4 In the greatness of your mercy
loose us from our chains: ▪
forgive the sins of all your people.

5 Make yourself known as our Saviour
and mighty Deliverer: ▪
save and help us that we may praise you.

6 Come now and dwell with us Lord Christ Jesus, ▪
hear our prayer and be with us always.

7 And when you come in your glory ▪
make us to be one with you
and to share the life of your kingdom. Amen.

Prayer

INTERCESSIONS AND THANKSGIVINGS

Pray for all who seek to grow in holiness during this season of Lent, for those who neglect the things of God in the business of daily life and for all who bring sin and suffering to others.

Give thanks that Jesus knows and understands human struggle against temptation, for the assurance that God's mercy knows no limit and for all acts of compassion and kindness that reveal Christ's Spirit at work in the world.

Almighty and everlasting God,
you hate nothing that you have made
and forgive the sins of all those who are penitent:
Create and make in us new and contrite hearts
that we, worthily lamenting our sins
and acknowledging our wretchedness,
may receive from you, the God of all mercy,
perfect remission and forgiveness;
through Jesus Christ our Lord. Amen.

or one of these prayers

Gracious and merciful God,
you see into the secret places of our hearts,
where we mourn our sins.
As we turn again to your grace,
receive our prayer
and look with mercy on our contrition.
Wash us from the stain of iniquity
and create a new and right spirit in us;
that we may declare your praise
and offer an acceptable sacrifice in these Lenten days;
through Christ Jesus, who bore our sins on the cross,
and now lives and reigns with you and the Holy Spirit,
one God, now and for ever. Amen.

Holy God,
our lives are laid open before you:
Rescue us from the chaos of sin
and through the death of your Son
bring us healing and make us whole
in Jesus Christ our Lord. Amen.

Alternative Collects

AN ENDING

Jesus, holy and strong,
by your fasting and temptation teach us self-denial;
control and discipline us
that we may learn to obey. Amen.

Prayer Book of New Zealand

The First Week of Lent

Preparation

A SENTENCE OF SCRIPTURE

Jesus taught, When you pray say, ... Do not bring us to the time of trial but rescue us from the Evil One.

Matthew 6: 13

A PRAYER OF PENITENCE

Wash away all my iniquity and cleanse me from my sin.
Lord, have mercy.

Against you, you only have I sinned and done what is evil in your sight.
Christ, have mercy.

Create in me a pure heart, O God, and renew a right spirit within me.
Lord, have mercy.

New Patterns of Worship

HYMN

Lord, who throughout these forty days
for us didst fast and pray,
teach us with Thee to mourn our sins,
and at thy side to stay.

As thou with Satan didst contend,
and didst the victory win,
O give us strength in thee to fight,
in thee to conquer sin.

As thirst and hunger thou didst bear,
so teach us, gracious Lord,
to die to self, and daily live
by thy most holy word.

And through these days of penitence,
and through thy Passion-tide,
yea, evermore, in life and death,
Lord Christ, with us abide.

Claudia F Hernaman (1838-98)

The Word of God

PSALM 25:1-9

For your name's sake, O Lord ▪
be merciful to my sin for it is great.

1 To you, O Lord, I lift up my soul;
O my God, in you I trust; ▪
let me not be put to shame;
let not my enemies triumph over me.
2 Let none who look to you be put to shame, ▪
but let the treacherous be shamed and frustrated.
3 Make me to know your ways, O Lord, ▪
and teach me your paths.
4 Lead me in your truth and teach me, ▪
for you are the God of my salvation;
for you have I hoped all the day long.
5 Remember, Lord, your compassion and love, ▪
for they are from everlasting.
6 Remember not the sins of my youth
or my transgressions, ▪
but think on me in your goodness, O Lord,
according to your steadfast love.
7 Gracious and upright is the Lord; ▪
therefore shall he teach sinners in the way.

8 He will guide the humble in doing right ▪
and teach his way to the lowly.
9 All the paths of the Lord are mercy and truth ▪
to those who keep his covenant and his testimonies.

A BIBLE READING

TESTED

Monday	*Ephesians 2: 1-10*
Tuesday	*1 Peter 3: 8-18a*
Wednesday	*Proverbs 30: 1-9*

ABRAHAM – MAN OF FAITH

Thursday	*Genesis 15: 1-6, 12-18*
Friday	*Romans 3: 21-31*
Saturday	*Romans 4: 1-12*

or

In those days Jesus came from Nazareth of Galilee and was baptized by John in the Jordan. And just as he was coming up out of the water, he saw the heavens torn apart and the Spirit descending like a dove on him. And a voice came from heaven, 'You are my Son, the Beloved; with you I am well pleased.' And the Spirit immediately drove him out into the wilderness. He was in the wilderness forty days, tempted by Satan; and he was with the wild beasts; and the angels waited on him. Now after John was arrested, Jesus came to Galilee, proclaiming the good news of God, and saying, 'The time is fulfilled, and the kingdom of God has come near; repent, and believe in the good news.'

Mark 1: 9-15

TE DEUM Part 2

7 You, Christ, are the King of glory ▪
the eternal Son of the Father.
8 When you took our flesh to set us free ▪
you humbly chose the virgin's womb.
9 You overcame the sting of death ▪
and opened the kingdom of heaven to all believers.
10 You are seated at God's right hand in glory: ▪
we believe that you will come to be our judge.
11 Come then, Lord, and help your people,
bought with the price of your own blood ▪
and bring us with your saints
to glory everlasting.

Prayer

INTERCESSIONS AND THANKSGIVINGS

Pray for those all whose find that the circumstances of their everyday lives test their faith, that Christian people may be strengthened to witness against the power of evil in society and for those who seek to gain their ends by evil means. Give thanks for the gifts God gives his people to enable them to resist the power of evil, for all the unsung heroes who in God's strength have made a difference to their communities, and for all that sets people free from pain and fear.

THE COLLECT OF LENT I

Almighty God,
whose Son Jesus Christ fasted forty days
  in the wilderness,
and was tempted as we are, yet without sin:
Give us grace to discipline ourselves
in obedience to your Spirit;
and, as you know our weakness,
so may we know your power to save;
through Jesus Christ our Lord. Amen.

or one of these prayers
God of our salvation,
your bow in the clouds proclaims your covenant
  with every living creature.
Fill us with your strength to resist the seductions
  of our foolish desires
and the tempter's vain delights,
that we may walk in obedience and righteousness,
rejoicing in you with an upright heart.
Grant this we pray through Jesus Christ our Lord.
Amen.

RCL Prayers altd.

Hear us, Lord Jesus,
when we ask for help to recognize temptation:
give us honesty to face it, strength to resist
and humility to give God the glory

Prayer Book of New Zealand

THE LORD'S PRAYER

God, grant us to know what is right,
do what is just
and follow your purpose in all things;
through Christ our Lord. Amen

Celebrating the Christian Year

The Second Week of Lent

Preparation

A SENTENCE OF SCRIPTURE

May I never boast of anything except the cross of our Lord Jesus Christ, by which the world is crucified to me, and I to the world.

Galatians 6: 14

A PRAYER OF PENITENCE

God of steadfast love,
out of your sheer goodness
you have brought us into a covenant with yourself.
But like your people of old
we disobey and break your laws,
even neglecting to draw near to you.
Turn us again, O God.
Forgive us our sin,
gather us in your embrace
and teach us the way that we should go;
for the sake of Jesus
who laid down his life as a ransom for all. Amen.

HYMN

The God of Abraham praise
who reigns enthroned above,
Ancient of everlasting Days,
and God of love:
To him uplift the voice,
at whose supreme command
from earth we rise and seek the joys
at his right hand.

He by himself has sworn,
I on his oath depend:
I shall, on eagles' wings upborne,
to heaven ascend;
I shall behold his face,
I shall his power adore
and sing the wonders of his grace
for evermore.

The God who reigns on high
the great archangels sing,
and 'Holy, Holy, Holy.' cry,
'almighty King,
who was, and is the same,
and evermore shall be:
eternal Father, great I AM,
we worship thee.'

The whole triumphant host
give thanks to God on high;
'hail, Father, Son, and Holy Ghost',
they ever cry:
hail, Abraham's God, and mine,
(I join the heavenly lays)
all might and majesty are thine,
and endless praise.

Daniel Ben Judah (fl 14th century),
Thomas Olivers (1725-99)

The Word of God

PSALM 147: 1-6

How deep are your counsels to me, O God! ▪
How great is the sum of them!

1 Alleluia.
How good it is to make music for our God, ▪
how joyful to honour him with praise.
2 The Lord builds up Jerusalem ▪
and gathers together the outcasts of Israel.
3 He heals the brokenhearted ▪
and binds up all their wounds.
4 He counts the number of the stars ▪
and calls them all by their names.
5 Great is our Lord and mighty in power; ▪
his wisdom is beyond all telling.
6 The Lord lifts up the poor, ▪
but casts down the wicked to the ground.

A BIBLE READING

ABRAHAM – MAN OF FAITH

Monday	*Genesis 21: 1-7*
Tuesday	*Hebrews 11: 1-3, 13-19*
Wednesday	*Mark 10: 32-34*

GOD'S TEMPLE

Thursday	*1 Kings 6: 1-14, 21-22*
Friday	*2 Chronicles 29: 1-11, 16-19*
Saturday	*Ezra 6: 1-16*

or

Then Jesus began to teach them that the Son of Man must undergo great suffering, and be rejected by the elders, the chief priests, and the scribes, and be killed, and after three days rise again. He said all this quite openly. And Peter took him aside and began to rebuke him. But turning and looking at his disciples, he rebuked Peter and said, 'Get behind me, Satan! For you are setting your mind not on divine things but on human things.' He called the crowd with his disciples, and said to them, 'If any want to become my followers, let them deny themselves and take up their cross and follow me. For those who want to save their life will lose it, and those who lose their life for my sake, and for the sake of the gospel, will save it. For what will it profit them to gain the whole world and forfeit their life? Indeed, what can they give in return for their life? Those who are ashamed of me and of my words in this adulterous and sinful generation, of them the Son of Man will also be ashamed when he comes in the glory of his Father with the holy angels.'

Mark 8: 31-38

A CANTICLE

GLORY AND HONOUR

Revelation 4: 11 and 5: 9,10 13b

1 Glory and honour and power ▪
are yours by right O Lord our God.
2 For you created all things ▪
and by your will they have their being.
3 Glory and honour and power ▪
are yours by right O Lamb for us slain;
4 For by your blood you ransomed us for God ▪
from every race and language
from every people and nation.
5 To make us a kingdom of priests ▪
to stand and serve before our God.
6 To him who sits on the throne and to the Lamb ▪
be praise and honour glory and might
for ever and ever. Amen.

Prayer

INTERCESSIONS AND THANKSGIVINGS

Pray for those drawn to Christian faith not yet willing to make a commitment to Christ, for those who teach theology, those preparing for baptism or confirmation and for those whose faith has been damaged by bad experiences of the Church.

Give thanks for scholars and translators, those who write books to encourage and stimulate the thinking of God's people, for those who publish and distribute them and for all that sets people free from pain and fear.

THE COLLECT OF LENT 2

Almighty God,
you show to those who are in error
the light of your truth
that they may return to the way of righteousness:
Grant to all those who are admitted
into the fellowship of Christ's religion,
that they may reject those things
that are contrary to their profession,
and follow all such things
as are agreeable to the same;
through our Lord Jesus Christ. Amen.

or one of these prayers

Eternal God, whose glory is always to have mercy:
Bring back all who have erred
and strayed from your ways,
lead them again to embrace with childlike faith
the truth of your Word and to hold it fast:
through Jesus Christ our Lord. Amen.

God,
you have made known your love
through the life and words of Jesus.
Help us to receive his teaching,
to find the fulness of that love
and bring its fragrance to others.

Prayer Book of New Zealand

THE LORD'S PRAYER

AN ENDING

Lord, you have created us for yourself,
you have called us into being:
all that we are, all that we do,
we give to you in love. Amen.

The Third Week of Lent

Preparation

A SENTENCE OF SCRIPTURE

Let the word of Christ dwell in you richly; teach and admonish one another in all wisdom; and with gratitude in your hearts sing psalms, hymns, and spiritual songs to God.

Colossians 3: 16

A PRAYER OF PENITENCE

Lord Jesus Christ,
as the earthly temple was defiled and needed cleansing,
so our bodies, temples of the Holy Spirit,
have become unclean
through our disobedience to your laws,
and our lives have not borne the harvest
for which you look.
We are truly sorry and repent of all our sins.
Purge, cleanse and sanctify us with your forgiving love;
and open our hearts to your word;
that we may become disciples worthy of your love
and bear fruit to your glory. Amen.

HYMN

Love Divine, all loves excelling,
joy of heaven to earth come down!
Fix in us thy humble dwelling,
all thy faithful mercies crown,
Jesu, thou art all compassion,
pure unbounded love thou art;
visit us with thy salvation,
enter every trembling heart.

Come, Almighty to deliver,
let us all thy grace receive!
Suddenly return, and never,
never more thy temples leave.
Thee we would be always blessing,
serve thee as thy hosts above,
pray, and praise thee without ceasing,
glory in thy perfect love.

Finish then thy new creation,
pure and spotless let us be;
let us see thy great salvation
perfectly restored in thee!
Changed from glory into glory,
till in heaven we take our place,
till we cast our crowns before thee,
lost in wonder, love and praise.

Charles Wesley (1707-88)

The Word of God

PSALM 84

Lord, I love the house of your habitation ▪
and the place where your glory abides.

1 How lovely is your dwelling place,
O Lord of hosts! ▪
My soul has a desire and longing
to enter the courts of the Lord;
my heart and my flesh rejoices in the living God.

2 The sparrow has found her a house
and the swallow a nest
where she may lay her young: ▪
at your altars, O Lord of hosts, my King and my God.

3 Blessed are they who dwell in your house: ▪
they will always be praising you.
4 Blessed are those whose strength is in you, ▪
in whose heart are the highways to Zion,
5 Who going through the barren valley find there
a spring, ▪
and the early rains will clothe it with blessing.
6 They will go from strength to strength ▪
and appear before God in Zion.
7 O Lord God of hosts, hear my prayer; ▪
listen, O God of Jacob.
8 Behold our defender, O God, ▪
and look upon the face of your anointed.
9 For one day in your courts ▪
is better than a thousand.
10 I would rather be a doorkeeper in the
house of my God ▪
than dwell in the tents of ungodliness.
11 For the Lord God is both sun and shield;
he will give grace and glory; ▪
no good thing shall the Lord withhold
from those who walk with integrity.
12 O Lord God of hosts, ▪
blessed are those who put their trust in you.

A BIBLE READING

CHRIST AND THE TEMPLE

Monday	*1 Corinthians 3: 10-23*
Tuesday	*Hebrews 9: 23-28*
Wednesday	*Mark 11: 15-19*

LIVING FOR CHRIST

Thursday	*Ephesians 1: 3-6*
Friday	*Ephesians 1: 7-14*
Saturday	*Numbers 21: 4-9*

or

The Passover of the Jews was near, and Jesus went up to Jerusalem. In the temple he found people selling cattle, sheep, and doves, and the money changers seated at their tables. Making a whip of cords, he drove all of them out of the temple, both the sheep and the cattle. He also poured out the coins of the money changers and overturned their tables. He told those who were selling the doves, 'Take these things out of here! Stop making my Father's house a marketplace!' His disciples remembered that it was written, 'Zeal for your house will consume me.' The Jews then said to him, 'What sign can you show us for doing this?' Jesus answered them, 'Destroy this temple, and in three days I will raise it up.' The Jews then said, 'This temple has been under construction for forty-six years, and will you raise it up in three days?' But he was speaking of the temple of his body. After he was raised from the dead, his disciples remembered that he had said this; and they believed the scripture and the word that Jesus had spoken.

John 2: 13-22

A CANTICLE

BLESS THE LORD

Song of the Three 29-34

1 Bless the Lord the God of our fathers ▪
sing his praise and exalt him for ever.

2 Bless his holy and glorious name ▪
sing his praise and exalt him for ever.

3 Bless him in his holy and glorious temple ▪
sing his praise and exalt him for ever.

4 Bless him who beholds the depth ▪
sing his praise and exalt him for ever.
5 Bless him seated between the cherubim ▪
sing his praise and exalt him for ever.
6 Bless him on the throne of his kingdom ▪
sing his praise and exalt him for ever.
7 Bless him in the heights of heaven ▪
sing his praise and exalt him for ever.
8 Bless the Father the Son and the Holy Spirit ▪
sing his praise and exalt him for ever.

Prayer

INTERCESSIONS AND THANKSGIVINGS

Pray for those conscious that they struggle with addictions, for those who seek to combat drug-traffickers and bring stability to shaken lives and for those called to bring the good news of the Gospel to those on the fringe of society.
Give thanks for aid-workers especially those who bring healing and hope, for those who sacrificially give their lives to the 'service of the poor', and for those who strive to bring wholeness to broken communities in places devastated through natural or human-caused disasters

THE COLLECT OF LENT 3

Merciful Lord,
Grant your people grace to withstand the temptations
of the world, the flesh and the devil
and with pure hearts and minds to follow you,
the only God;
through Jesus Christ our Lord. Amen.

or one of these prayers

Holy God,
the folly of the cross mocks our human wisdom
and the weakness of the crucified
puts worldly power to shame:
By the power that flows from the Saviour's death
and resurrection
may your people be raised up from the death of sin
to become living temples of your glory.
Grant this through Jesus Christ our liberator from sin.
Amen.

Lord Jesus,
as we search the scriptures
patiently and reverently,
may we be led to you,
the Word made flesh:
for you have the words of eternal life. Amen.

Prayer Book of New Zealand

THE LORD'S PRAYER

AN ENDING

Eternal God,
give us insight,
to discern your will for us,
to give up what harms us
and to seek the perfection we are promised
in Jesus Christ our Lord.

Alternative Collects

The Fourth Week of Lent

Preparation

A SENTENCE OF SCRIPTURE

Jesus said, Unless a grain of wheat falls into the earth and dies, it remains a single grain; but if it dies it bears much fruit.

John 12: 24

A PRAYER OF PENITENCE

Merciful and dependable Lord,
you reach out to us in mercy
even when we rebel and refuse to listen to your call.
We confess that we prefer to walk in disobedience
rather than in the way of your holy laws.
We seek your forgiveness
and pray that you will soften our hearts
with the warmth of your saving love,
that we may know your Son alive within us,
redeeming us,
and raising us up into your eternal presence.
We pray in his name who was lifted up on the cross
to draw men and women everywhere to him. Amen .

RCL Prayers altd

HYMN

O my Saviour, lifted
from the earth for me,
draw me, in thy mercy,
nearer unto thee.

Speed these lagging footsteps,
melt this heart of ice,
as I scan the marvels
of thy Sacrifice.

Lift my earth-bound longings,
fix them, Lord, above;
draw me with the magnet
of thy mighty love.

Lord, thine arms are stretching
ever far and wide,
to enfold thy children
to thy loving side.

And I come, O Jesus,
dare I turn away?
No, thy love hath conquered,
and I come today:

Bringing all my burdens,
sorrow, sin and care,
at thy feet I lay them,
and I leave them there.

W. Walsham How (1823-97)

The Word of God

PSALM 107: 1-9

The Lord shall refresh my soul ■
and guide me in the paths of righteousness
for his name's sake.

1 O give thanks to the Lord, for he is gracious, ■
for his steadfast love endures for ever.
2 Let the redeemed of the Lord say this, ■
those he redeemed from the hand of the enemy,

3 And gathered out of the lands
    from the east and from the west, ▪
from the north and from the south.
4 Some went astray in desert wastes ▪
and found no path to a city to dwell in.
5 Hungry and thirsty, ▪
their soul was fainting within them.
6 So they cried to the Lord in their trouble ▪
and he delivered them from their distress.
7 He set their feet on the right way ▪
till they came to a city to dwell in.
8 Let them give thanks to the Lord for his goodness ▪
and the wonders he does for his children.
9 For he satisfies the longing soul ▪
and fills the hungry soul with good.

A BIBLE READING

LIVING FOR CHRIST

Monday	*Hebrews 3: 1-6*
Tuesday	*1 Corinthians 10: 6-13*
Wednesday	*John 8: 12-20*
Thursday	*Isaiah 30: 15-18*
Friday	*Hebrews 4: 14 - 5: 4*
Saturday	*Habakkuk 3: 2-13*

or

Jesus said, Just as Moses lifted up the serpent in the wilderness, so must the Son of Man be lifted up, that whoever believes in him may have eternal life. For God so loved the world that he gave his only Son, so that everyone who believes in him may not perish but may have eternal life. Indeed, God did not send the Son into the world to condemn the world, but in order that the world might be saved through him. Those who believe in him are not condemned; but those who do not believe are condemned already, because they have not believed in the name of the only Son of God. And this is the judgment, that the light has come into the world, and people loved darkness rather than light because their deeds were evil. For all who do evil hate the light and do not come to the light, so that their deeds may not be exposed. But those who do what is true come to the light, so that it may be clearly seen that their deeds have been done in God.

John 3: 14-21

A CANTICLE

URBS FORTITUDINIS

Isaiah 26: 1-4, 7, 8

1 We have a strong city ▪
salvation will God appoint for walls and bulwarks.

2 Open ye the gates ▪
that the righteous nation which keepeth the truth
may enter in.

3 Thou wilt keep him in perfect peace
whose mind is stayed on thee ▪
because he trusteth in thee.

4 Trust ye in the Lord for ever ▪
for our rock of ages is the Lord.

5 The way of the just is uprightness ▪
thou that art upright dost direct the path of the just.

6 Yea in the way of thy judgements O Lord
have we waited for thee ▪
the desire of our soul is to thy Name
and to the remembrance of thee.

Prayer

INTERCESSIONS AND THANKSGIVINGS

Pray for those who are unaware of the Good News of forgiveness and meaning in life, for those are called to proclaim the Gospel in a society that often sees no need to listen, for those seeking to bear their witness to Jesus by lives renewed and refreshed by the Holy Spirit, and for parents, especially single mothers, seeking to bring up their children in the fear and nurture of the Lord.

Give thanks for all opportunities to show love and compassion to others, for those who are at this time seeking baptism or the gifts of the Holy Spirit in confirmation and for those whose Christian lives and witness have encouraged us in our discipleship

THE COLLECT OF LENT 4

Lord God
whose blessed Son our Saviour
gave his back to the smiters
and did not hide his face from shame:
Give us grace to endure the sufferings
of this present time
with sure confidence in the glory that shall be revealed;
through Jesus Christ our Lord. Amen.

or one of these prayers

O God,
with steadfast love you draw us to yourself:
Strengthen us to bring forth the fruit of the Spirit,
that through life and death
we may live in your Son Jesus Christ,
whom with you and the Holy Spirit
we worship and praise,
one God, now and ever. Amen

Lutheran Renewing Worship

God of the hungry,
make us hunger and thirst for the right,
till our thirst for justice has been satisfied
poverty made history
and hunger has gone from the earth.
We ask it in the name of Jesus. Amen.

Prayer Book of New Zealand altd.

THE LORD'S PRAYER

AN ENDING

Lifted up from the earth,
Lord Jesus, you are light and life.
Raise us up to walk each day with you in this life
and bring us at the last to the fulness of your kingdom.

The Fifth Week of Lent

Preparation

A SENTENCE OF SCRIPTURE

Jesus said: 'I, when I am lifted up from the earth, will draw all people to myself.'

John 12: 32

A PRAYER OF PENITENCE

The gospel calls us to turn away from sin and be faithful to Christ. As we offer ourselves to him in penitence and faith, we renew our confidence and trust in his mercy.

Father, you raise the dead to life in the Spirit:
Lord, have mercy.

Lord Jesus, you bring pardon and peace to the sinner:
Christ, have mercy.

Comforter, you bring light to those in darkness:
Lord, have mercy.

HYMN

We sing the praise of him who died,
of him who died upon the Cross;
the sinner's hope let men deride;
for this we count the world but loss.

Inscribed upon the Cross we see
in shining letters, 'God is love';
he bears our sins upon the Tree;
he brings us mercy from above.

The Cross! It takes our guilt away;
it holds the fainting spirit up;
it cheers with hope the gloomy day,
and sweetens every bitter cup.

It makes the coward spirit brave,
and nerves the feeble arm for fight;
it takes its terror from the grave,
and gilds the bed of death with light:

The balm of life, the cure of woe,
the measure and the pledge of love,
the sinner's refuge here below,
the angels' theme in heaven above.

Thomas Kelly (1769-1854)

The Word of God

PSALM 31: 1-5

Though I walk through the valley of the shadow of death ▪
I will fear no evil.

1 In you, O Lord, have I taken refuge;
let me never be put to shame; ▪
deliver me in your righteousness.
2 Incline your ear to me; ▪
make haste to deliver me.
3 Be my strong rock, a fortress to save me,
for you are my rock and my stronghold; ▪
guide me, and lead me for your name's sake.
4 Take me out of the net
that they have laid secretly for me, ▪
for you are my strength.
5 Into your hands I commend my spirit, ▪
for you have redeemed me, O Lord God of truth.

THE GLORY OF THE CROSS

Monday	*2 Corinthians 3: 4-11*
Tuesday	*Acts 2: 14-24*
Wednesday	*John 12: 34-50*
Thursday	*Philippians 2: 1-11*
Friday	*Philippians 2: 12-18*
Saturday	*Mark 10: 32-34, 46-52*

or

Now among those who went up to worship at the festival were some Greeks. They came to Philip, who was from Bethsaida in Galilee, and said to him, 'Sir, we wish to see Jesus.' Philip went and told Andrew; then Andrew and Philip went and told Jesus. Jesus answered them, 'The hour has come for the Son of Man to be glorified. Very truly, I tell you, unless a grain of wheat falls into the earth and dies, it remains just a single grain; but if it dies, it bears much fruit. Those who love their life lose it, and those who hate their life in this world will keep it for eternal life. Whoever serves me must follow me, and where I am, there will my servant be also. Whoever serves me, the Father will honour.

'Now my soul is troubled. And what should I say – "Father, save me from this hour"? No, it is for this reason that I have come to this hour. Father, glorify your name.' Then a voice came from heaven, 'I have glorified it, and I will glorify it again.' The crowd standing there heard it and said that it was thunder. Others said, 'An angel has spoken to him.' Jesus answered, 'This voice has come for your sake, not for mine. Now is the judgment of this world; now the ruler of this world will be driven out. And I, when I am lifted up from the earth, will draw all people to myself.' He said this to indicate the kind of death he was to die.

John 12: 20-33

A CANTICLE

TE DEUM part 3

13 Save your people, Lord, and bless your inheritance ▪
govern and uphold them now and always.
14 Day by day we bless you ▪
we praise your name for ever
15 Keep us today, Lord, from all sin ▪
have mercy on us, Lord, have mercy.
16 Lord, show us your love and mercy ▪
for we put our trust in you.
17 In you, Lord, is our hope ▪
let us never be put to shame.

Prayer

INTERCESSIONS AND THANKSGIVINGS

Pray for all who are searching for meaning in life, that the outreach of the Church at this season may bring many to faith in the one crucified to draw all people to him. Pray for all who minister to the bereaved and those damaged by ministry that has been insensitive though well-meaning. Pray that for all who at the climax of this Passiontide will be baptized and brought into the family of the church.
Give thanks for faith, for the victory of the Passion and the hope which the Easter message brings.

THE COLLECT OF LENT 5

Most merciful God,
who by the death and resurrection
of your Son Jesus Christ
delivered and saved the world:
Grant that by faith in him who suffered on the cross,
we may triumph in the power of his victory;
through Jesus Christ our Lord. Amen.

or one of these prayers

Jesus, they hung you on a cross
because you love sinners.
Save us from our self-righteousness
and from our contempt for those who differ from us.

Prayer Book of New Zealand

God of suffering and glory,
you gave up your Son out of love for the world:
Lead us to ponder the mysteries of his passion,
and to wonder at his obedience
even to death on the cross.
Write your laws in our hearts
that in life we may not stray from you
and in life and death may know the eternal peace
which is ours through the blood
of Jesus Christ our Saviour, shed for us.
We ask it in his name. Amen.

THE LORD'S PRAYER

AN ENDING

Saviour of the world,
by your cross and passion you have redeemed us,
save and help us, we humbly pray. Amen.

Holy Week: Monday, Tuesday and Wednesday

Preparation

A SENTENCE OF SCRIPTURE

This is love: not that we loved God, but that he loved us and sent his son as an atoning sacrifice for our sins.

1 John 4: 10 (TNIV)

A PRAYER OF PENITENCE

Gracious and merciful God,
as in heart and mind we see Jesus in his passion,
we confess our sins of thought, word and deed,
and our failure to do what we know we should.
Our sins with those of all humankind
brought him to the Cross:
we are indeed sorry
and are overwhelmed by your wonderful love
by which we receive forgiveness.
Guide and strengthen us to amend our lives
and become disciples worthy of your love.
We ask this through him who suffered and died for us
and now lives with you in the fulness of glory,
Jesus Christ our Lord. Amen.

HYMN

Praise to the Holiest in the height,
and in the depth be praise:
in all his words most wonderful,
most sure in all his ways.

O loving wisdom of our God!
when all was sin and shame,

a second Adam to the fight
and to the rescue came.

O wisest love! that flesh and blood,
which did in Adam fail,
should strive afresh against the foe,
should strive and should prevail;

And that a higher gift than grace
should flesh and blood refine,
God's presence and his very self,
an essence all-divine.

O generous love! that he, who smote
in Man for man the foe,
the double agony in Man
for man should undergo;

And in the garden secretly,
and on the Cross on high,
should teach his brethren, and inspire
to suffer and to die.

Praise to the Holiest in the height,
and in the depth be praise:
in all his words most wonderful,
most sure in all his ways.

John Henry Newman (1801-90)

The Word of God

PSALM 55: 1-6, 22-24

You are my helper and deliverer ▪
O Lord, do not delay.

1 Hear my prayer, O God; ▪
hide not yourself from my petition.

2 Give heed to me and answer me; ▪
I am restless in my complaining.
3 I am alarmed at the voice of the enemy ▪
and at the clamour of the wicked;
4 For they would bring down evil upon me ▪
and are set against me in fury.
5 My heart is disquieted within me, ▪
and the terrors of death have fallen upon me.
6 Fearfulness and trembling are come upon me, ▪
and a horrible dread has overwhelmed me.
22 My companion stretched out his hands
against his friend ▪
and has broken his covenant;
23 His speech was softer than butter,
though war was in his heart; ▪
his words were smoother than oil,
yet are they naked swords.
24 Cast your burden upon the Lord
and he will sustain you, ▪
and will not let the righteous fall for ever.

A BIBLE READING

THE MESSIAH IN JERUSALEM

Monday	*John 12: 1-11*
Tuesday	*John 12: 20-36*
Wednesday	*John 13: 21-32*

or

Six days before the Passover Jesus came to Bethany, the home of Lazarus, whom he had raised from the dead. There they gave a dinner for him. Martha served, and Lazarus was one of those at the table with him. Mary took a pound of costly perfume made of pure nard, anointed Jesus' feet, and wiped them with her hair. The house was filled with the fragrance of the perfume. But Judas Iscariot, one of his disciples (the one who was about to betray him), said, 'Why was this perfume not sold for three hundred denarii and the money given to the poor?' (He said this not because he cared about the poor, but because he was a thief; he kept the common purse and used to steal what was put into it.) Jesus said, 'Leave her alone. She bought it so that she might keep it for the day of my burial. You always have the poor with you, but you do not always have me.'

When the great crowd of the Jews learned that he was there, they came not only because of Jesus but also to see Lazarus, whom he had raised from the dead. So the chief priests planned to put Lazarus to death as well, since it was on account of him that many of the Jews were deserting and were believing in Jesus.

John 12: 1-11

A CANTICLE

A SONG OF PETER

1 Peter 2: 21b-25

1 Christ suffered for us, leaving us an example, ▪
that we should follow in his steps.

2 He committed no sin,
no guile was found on his lips, ▪
when he was reviled, he did not revile in turn.

3 When he suffered, he did not threaten, ▪
but he trusted himself to God who judges justly.

4 Christ himself bore our sins in his body
on the tree, ▪
that we might die to sin and live to righteousness.

5 By his wounds, we have been healed,
for we were straying like sheep, ▪
but have now returned to the shepherd
and guardian of our souls.

Prayer

INTERCESSIONS AND THANKSGIVINGS

Pray for all who share in keeping Holy Week, for those who suffer today in the Holy Land and all for whom the way of the Cross is an everyday experience. Pray for all preparing for baptism or confirmation at the climax of this season. Give thanks for Christ's suffering and his victory, and the hope that it brings to this living in the shadow of death. Give thanks for the whole Catholic Church in all its branches which brings this Good News to people today.

A COLLECT

God of steadfast love,
light of the blind and liberator of the oppressed:
we see your holy purpose
in the tender compassion of Jesus,
who calls us into new and living friendship with you.
May we, who take shelter in the shadow of his wings,
be filled with the grace of his caring love;
may we who stumble in selfish darkness see your glory
in the light of his self-giving.
We ask this through him who suffering is victorious,
Jesus Christ our Saviour.

RCL Prayers

or this prayer

Almighty God,
your name is glorified
in the anguish of your Son's death:
Grant us courage and empower us in witness,
so that the world may recognize
in the scandal of the cross
the mystery of reconciliation.
We ask this in name of Jesus,
who embodied a wisdom and love
beyond human understanding.

RCL Prayers altd.

THE LORD'S PRAYER

AN ENDING

Saviour of the world,
may your cross stand as a sign of the power
that conquers pride and confounds the wisdom of the world. Amen.

Holy Week: Maundy Thursday, Good Friday, and Holy Saturday

Preparation

A SENTENCE OF SCRIPTURE

Christ humbled himself and became obedient to the point of death – even death on a cross. Therefore God also highly exalted him and gave him the name that is above every name.

Philippians 2: 8-9

A PRAYER OF PENITENCE

Merciful God,
we confess that we have sinned against you
in thought, word and deed,
by what we have done,
and by what we have left undone.
We have not loved you
with our whole heart, mind and strength;
we have not loved our neighbours as ourselves.
In your mercy forgive what we have been,
help us to amend what we are,
and direct what we shall be,
so that we may delight in your will
and walk in your ways,
to the glory of your holy name. Amen.

HYMN

When I survey the wondrous cross
on which the prince of glory died,
my richest gain I count as loss,
and pour contempt on all my pride.

Forbid it, Lord, that I should boast
save in the cross of Christ my God;
the very things that charm me most –
I sacrifice them to his blood.

See from his head, his hands, his feet,
sorrow and love flow mingled down:
when did such love and sorrow meet,
or thorns compose so rich a crown?

Were the whole realm of nature mine,
that were an offering far too small;
love so amazing, so divine,
demands my soul, my life, my all!

Isaac Watts (1674-1728)

The Word of God

PSALM 22: 1-11

Answer me, O Lord, for your love is kind ▪
in your compassion, turn to me.

1 My God, my God, why have you forsaken me, ▪
and are so far from my salvation,
from the words of my distress?
2 O my God, I cry in the daytime,
but you do not answer; ▪
and by night also, but I find no rest.
3 Yet you are the Holy One, ▪
enthroned upon the praises of Israel.
4 Our forebears trusted in you; ▪
they trusted, and you delivered them.
5 They cried out to you and were delivered; ▪
they put their trust in you and were not confounded.
6 But as for me, I am a worm and no man, ▪
scorned by all and despised by the people.

7 All who see me laugh me to scorn; ▪
they curl their lips and wag their heads, saying,
8 'He trusted in the Lord; let him deliver him; ▪
let him deliver him, if he delights in him.'
9 But it is you that took me out of the womb ▪
and laid me safe upon my mother's breast.
10 On you was I cast ever since I was born; ▪
you are my God even from my mother's womb.
11 Be not far from me, for trouble is near at hand ▪
and there is none to help.

A BIBLE READING

CHRIST CRUCIFIED

Thursday	*John 13: 1-17,31b-35*
Friday	*Mark 15: 1-41*
Saturday	*Mark 15; 42-47*

or

The soldiers led Jesus into the courtyard of the palace (that is, the governor's headquarters); and they called together the whole cohort. And they clothed him in a purple cloak; and after twisting some thorns into a crown, they put it on him. And they began saluting him, 'Hail, King of the Jews!' They struck his head with a reed, spat upon him, and knelt down in homage to him. After mocking him, they stripped him of the purple cloak and put his own clothes on him. Then they led him out to crucify him. They compelled a passer-by, who was coming in from the country, to carry his cross; it was Simon of Cyrene, the father of Alexander and Rufus. Then they brought Jesus to the place called Golgotha (which means the place of a skull). And they offered him wine mixed with myrrh; but he did not take it. And they crucified him, and divided his clothes among them, casting lots to decide what each should take. It was nine o'clock in the morning when they crucified him. The inscription of the charge against him read, 'The King of the Jews.' And with him they crucified two bandits, one on his right and one on his left. Those who passed by derided him, shaking their heads and saying, 'Aha! You who would destroy the temple and build it in three days, save yourself, and come down from the cross!' In the same way the chief priests, along with the scribes, were also mocking him among themselves and saying, 'He saved others; he cannot save himself. Let the Messiah, the King of Israel, come down from the cross now, so that we may see and believe.' Those who were crucified with him also taunted him. When it was noon, darkness came over the whole land until three in the afternoon. At three o'clock Jesus cried out with a loud voice, 'Eloi, Eloi, lema sabachthani?' which means, 'My God, my God, why have you forsaken me?' When some of the bystanders heard it, they said, 'Listen, he is calling for Elijah.' And someone ran, filled a sponge with sour wine, put it on a stick, and gave it to him to drink, saying, 'Wait, let us see whether Elijah will come to take him down.' Then Jesus gave a loud cry and breathed his last. And the curtain of the temple was torn in two, from top to bottom. Now when the centurion, who stood facing him, saw that in this way he breathed his last, he said, 'Truly this man was God's Son!'

Mark 15: 16-39

A SONG OF LAMENTATION

Lamentations 1: 12, 16a; 3: 19, 22-28, 31-33

1 Is it nothing to you, all you who pass by? ▪
Look and see if there is any sorrow like my sorrow;
2 Which was brought upon me, ▪
which the Lord inflicted
on the day of his fierce anger.
3 For these things I weep;
my eyes flow with tears; ▪
for a comforter is far from me,
one to revive my courage;
4 Remember my affliction and my bitterness, ▪
the wormwood and the gall!
5 The steadfast love of the Lord never ceases, ▪
his mercies never come to an end;
6 They are new every morning; ▪
great is your faithfulness.
7 'The Lord is my portion', says my soul, ▪
'therefore I will hope in him.'
8 The Lord is good to those who wait for him, ▪
to the soul that seeks him.
9 It is good that we should wait quietly ▪
for the salvation of the Lord.
10 It is good to bear the yoke in our youth; ▪
to sit alone in silence when he has imposed it.
11 For the Lord will not reject for ever, ▪
though he causes grief, he will have compassion,
12 According to the abundance of his steadfast love; ▪
for he does not willingly afflict or grieve anyone.

Prayer

INTERCESSIONS AND THANKSGIVINGS

Pray for all God's hurting children in this weary world. Pray for peace for all peoples in Christ Jesus. Pray for the unity of all Christ's followers who draw near to the foot of the cross.

Give thanks for Christ's suffering and his victory. Give thanks for new creation in Christ and all gifts of healing and forgiveness.

A COLLECT

Gracious and loving God,
on the cross your Son embraced death
even as he had embraced life,
with faithfulness and good courage.
Grant that we who have been reborn
in the blood and water
which flowed from his wounded side
may hold fast to our faith in him
and in all times find mercy in him,
our Saviour and Lord,
whom with you and the Holy Spirit
we worship and praise,
one God, now and for ever. Amen.

Lutheran Renewal Worship altd.

or this prayer

Eternal God,
in the coss of Jesus we see the cost of our sin
and the depth of your love:
In humble hope and fear
may we place at his feet
all that we have and all that we are,
through Jesus Christ our Lord. Amen.

Alternative Collects

THE LORD'S PRAYER

AN ENDING

Saviour of the world,
by your cross and passion you have redeemed us,
save and help us, we humbly pray. Amen.

The First Week of Easter

Preparation

A SENTENCE OF SCRIPTURE

For I handed on to you as of first importance what I in turn had received: that Christ died for our sins in accordance with the scriptures, and that he was buried, and that he was raised on the third day in accordance with the scriptures.

1 Corinthians 15: 3-4

A PRAYER OF PENITENCE

Almighty God,
in raising Jesus from the tomb,
you destroyed the power of death.
Hear us as we confess our failure
to live by the good news of the resurrection.
Grant us the radiant power of your grace:
forgive, heal and renew us,
so that we may know and share the joy of life abundant,
given in Jesus Christ, our risen Lord.

Lutheran Renewal Worship altd.

HYMN

Jesus Christ is risen today, Alleluia!
our triumphant holy day, Alleluia!
who did once, upon the Cross, Alleluia!
suffer to redeem our loss. Alleluia!

Hymns of praise then let us sing, Alleluia!
unto Christ, our heavenly King, Alleluia!
who endured the Cross and grave, Alleluia!
sinners to redeem and save. Alleluia!

But the pains that he endured, Alleluia!
our salvation have procured; Alleluia!
now above the sky he's King, Alleluia!
where the angels ever sing. Alleluia!

Lyra Davidica 1708

The Word of God

PSALM 16: 5-11

The Lord is risen from the tomb ▪
Alleluia.

5 O Lord, you are my portion and my cup; ▪
it is you who uphold my lot.
6 My boundaries enclose a pleasant land; ▪
indeed, I have a goodly heritage.
7 I will bless the Lord who gives me counsel; ▪
my heart teaches me, night after night.
8 I have set the Lord always before me; ▪
because he is at my right hand I shall not fall.
9 My heart, therefore, is glad and my spirit rejoices; ▪
my body also shall rest in hope.
10 For you will not abandon me to the grave, ▪
nor let your holy one see the Pit.
11 You will show me the path of life; ▪
in your presence there is fullness of joy,
and in your right hand are pleasures for evermore.

A BIBLE READING

CHRIST THE LORD IS RISEN

Monday	*1 Corinthians 15: 35-49*
Tuesday	*1 Corinthians 15: 50-58*
Wednesday	*Mark 16: 1-8*
Thursday	*Acts 2: 42-47*
Friday	*Acts 4: 23-31*
Saturday	*John 12: 44-50*

or

Early on the first day of the week, while it was still dark, Mary Magdalene came to the tomb and saw that the stone had been removed from the tomb. So she ran and went to Simon Peter and the other disciple, the one whom Jesus loved, and said to them, 'They have taken the Lord out of the tomb, and we do not know where they have laid him.' Then Peter and the other disciple set out and went toward the tomb. The two were running together, but the other disciple outran Peter and reached the tomb first. He bent down to look in and saw the linen wrappings lying there, but he did not go in. Then Simon Peter came, following him, and went into the tomb. He saw the linen wrappings lying there, and the cloth that had been on Jesus' head, not lying with the linen wrappings but rolled up in a place by itself. Then the other disciple, who reached the tomb first, also went in, and he saw and believed; for as yet they did not understand the scripture, that he must rise from the dead. Then the disciples returned to their homes.

John 20: 1-10

A CANTICLE

THE EASTER ANTHEMS

1 Cor 5: 7, 8; Rom 6: 9-11; 1 Cor 15: 20-22

1 Christ our passover has been sacrificed for us ▪
therefore let us celebrate the feast.

2 Not with the old leaven of corruption
and wickedness ▪
but with the unleavened bread of sincerity and truth.

3 Christ once raised from the dead dies no more ▪
death has no more dominion over him.

4 In dying he died to sin once for all ▪
in living he lives to God.

5 See yourselves therefore as dead to sin ▪
and alive to God in Jesus Christ our Lord.

6 Christ has been raised from the dead ▪
the first fruits of those who sleep.

7 For as by man came death ▪
by man has come also the resurrection of the dead.

8 For as in Adam all die ▪
even so in Christ shall all be made alive.

Prayer

INTERCESSIONS AND THANKSGIVINGS

Pray for the Church worldwide – the community of the resurrection, for courageous witness and bold proclamation, and for all who are in pain or grieving over loved ones who have died, that they may know the comfort of God's love and the assurance of Easter hope.

Rejoice in Christ's victory over sin, evil and death. Give thanks for our foretaste of eternal life in baptism and eucharist.

THE COLLECT OF EASTER

Almighty God,
through your only-begotten Son Jesus Christ
you have overcome death
and opened to us the gate of everlasting life:
Grant that, as by your grace going before us
you put into our minds good desires,
so by your continual help
we may bring them to good effect;
through Jesus Christ our Risen Lord
who is alive and reigns with you and the Holy Spirit,
one God, now and for ever. Amen.

or one of these prayers

Living God,
for our redemption you gave your only-begotten Son
to the death of the cross,
and by his glorious resurrection
have delivered us from the power of our enemy:
grant us so to die daily unto sin,
that we may evermore live with him
in the joy of his risen life;
through Jesus Christ our Lord. Amen.

Post Communion Prayer

Mighty God,
in whom we know the power of redemption,
you stand among us in the shadows of our time.
In every sorrow and trial
uphold us with a vision of that final morning
when in the glorious presence of your risen Son,
we will share in his resurrection,
redeemed and restored to fulness of life;
through Jesus Christ our Risen Lord. Amen.

RCL Prayers altd.

THE LORD'S PRAYER

AN ENDING

May the love of the Cross,
the power of the Resurrection,
and the presence of the living Lord
be with us always. Amen.

The Second Week of Easter

Preparation

A SENTENCE OF SCRIPTURE

Jesus came and stood among the disciples and said, 'Peace be with you.' Then the disciples rejoiced when they saw the Lord.

John 20: 19, 20

A PRAYER OF PENITENCE

We come seeking forgiveness
for all we have failed to be and do
as members of Christ's body.
Loving and all-seeing God, forgive us.
Give us your peace that we may rejoice and be glad:
for Christ has risen bringing reconciliation with you
for all who turn to you.
We ask, trusting your love, through Jesus Christ our Lord.

Prayer Book of New Zealand altd.

HYMN

Thine be the glory, risen, conquering Son,
endless is the victory thou o'er death hast won;
angels in bright raiment rolled the stone away,
kept the folded grave-clothes where thy body lay:
Thine be the glory, risen, conquering Son,
endless is the victory thou o'er death hast won.

Lo, Jesus meets us, risen from the tomb;
lovingly he greets us, scatters fear and gloom;
let the Church with gladness hymns of triumph sing,
for her Lord now liveth, death hath lost its sting:

No more we doubt thee, glorious Prince of Life;
life is nought without thee: aid us in our strife;
make us more than conquerors
through thy deathless love;
bring us safe through Jordan to thy home above.

French. Edmond Budry (1854-1932)

The Word of God

PSALM 123

The Lord has been mindful of us and he will bless us. ▪ *Alleluia.*

1 To you I lift up my eyes, ▪
to you that are enthroned in the heavens.
2 As the eyes of servants look to the hand
of their master, ▪
or the eyes of a maid to the hand of her mistress,
3 So our eyes wait upon the Lord our God, ▪
until he have mercy upon us.
4 Have mercy upon us, O Lord,
have mercy upon us, ▪
for we have had more than enough of contempt.
5 Our soul has had more than enough
of the scorn of the arrogant, ▪
and of the contempt of the proud.

A BIBLE READING

RESURRECTION FAITH

Monday	*1 John 2: 3-11*
Tuesday	*1 John 2: 12-17*
Wednesday	*Mark 12: 18-27*
Thursday	*1 John 2: 18-25*
Friday	*1 John 2: 26-28*
Saturday	*Luke 22: 24-30*

or

When it was evening on that day, the first day of the week, and the doors of the house where the disciples had met were locked for fear of the Jews, Jesus came and stood among them and said, 'Peace be with you.' After he said this, he showed them his hands and his side. Then the disciples rejoiced when they saw the Lord. Jesus said to them again, 'Peace be with you. As the Father has sent me, so I send you.' When he had said this, he breathed on them and said to them, 'Receive the Holy Spirit. If you forgive the sins of any, they are forgiven them; if you retain the sins of any, they are retained.'

But Thomas (who was called the Twin), one of the twelve, was not with them when Jesus came. So the other disciples told him, 'We have seen the Lord.' But he said to them, 'Unless I see the mark of the nails in his hands, and put my finger in the mark of the nails and my hand in his side, I will not believe.'

A week later his disciples were again in the house, and Thomas was with them. Although the doors were shut, Jesus came and stood among them and said, 'Peace be with you.' Then he said to Thomas, 'Put your finger here and see my hands. Reach out your hand and put it in my side. Do not doubt but believe.' Thomas answered him, 'My Lord and my God!' Jesus said to him, 'Have you believed because you have seen me? Blessed are those who have not seen and yet have come to believe.'

John 20: 19-29

A SONG OF FAITH

Based on 1 Peter 1: 3-4, 18-21

1 Blessed be the God and Father ▪
of our Lord Jesus Christ!

2 By his great mercy we have been born anew
to a living hope ▪
through the resurrection of Jesus Christ
from the dead.

3 Into an inheritance that is imperishable,
undefiled and unfading, ▪
kept in heaven for us.

4 Who are being protected by the power of God ▪
through faith for a salvation,
ready to be revealed in the last time.

5 Ransomed from the futile ways of your ancestors ▪
not with perishable things like silver or gold

6 But with the precious blood of Christ ▪
like that of a lamb without spot or stain.

7 Through him we have confidence in God, ▪
who raised him from the dead and gave him glory,
so that our faith and hope are set on God.

Prayer

INTERCESSIONS AND THANKSGIVINGS

Pray for those called and sent as ministers of reconciliation to bring all God's children into his peace. Pray for those who find faith and commitment difficult.

Give thanks for the those who boldly witness to the power of the resurrection by lives dedicated to the service of others. Give thanks for all who have encouraged us in our pilgrimage in faith.

THE COLLECT OF EASTER 2

Almighty Father,
you have given your only Son to die for our sins
and to rise again for our justification:
Grant us so to put away the leaven
of malice and wickedness
that we may always serve you
in pureness of living and truth;
through the merits of your Son Jesus Christ our Lord.
Amen

or one of these prayers
Jesus, we believe in you;
all that we heard is true.
You break the bread,
we recognize you.
You are the fire that burns within us,
use us to bring light to the world. Amen.

Prayer Book of New Zealand

Risen Christ,
for whom no door is locked, no entrance barred:
open the doors of our hearts,
that we may seek the good of others
and walk the joyful road of sacrifice and peace,
to the praise of God the Father. Amen.

Alternative Collects

THE LORD'S PRAYER

The God of peace, who brought again from the dead our Lord Jesus, the great shepherd of the sheep, by the blood of the eternal covenant, make us perfect in everything good to do his will, working among us that which is well-pleasing in his sight, through Jesus Christ, to whom be glory for ever and ever.

Hebrews 13; 20, 21

The Third Week of Easter

Preparation

A SENTENCE OF SCRIPTURE

Jesus himself stood among his disciples and said to them, 'Peace be with you.'

Luke 24: 36

A PRAYER OF PENITENCE

God of all mercy;
we confess that we have sinned against you.
We have not honoured you in ourselves,
in one another and in the world you have made.
Reach out your saving arm
and rescue us from our sin.
Forgive, restore and strengthen us
through our risen Lord Jesus Christ,
that we may dwell in your love
and serve only your will
for your people and for your creation. Amen.

HYMN

Jesu, stand among us
in thy risen power;
let this time of worship
be a hallowed hour.

Breathe thy Holy Spirit
into every heart;
bid the fears and sorrows
from each soul depart.

Thus with quickened footsteps
we will go our way,
watching for the dawning
of the eternal day.

William Pennefather (1816-73)

The Word of God

PSALM 116: 10-17

My soul is athirst for God even for the living God. ■
Alleluia.

10 How shall I repay the Lord ■
for all the benefits he has given to me?
11 I will lift up the cup of salvation ■
and call upon the name of the Lord.
12 I will pay my vows to the Lord ■
in the presence of all his people.
13 Precious in the sight of the Lord ■
is the death of his faithful servants.
14 O Lord I am your servant ■
your servant, the child of your handmaid;
you have freed me from my bonds.
15 I will offer to you a sacrifice of thanksgiving ■
and call upon the name of the Lord.
16 I will fulfil my vows to the Lord ■
in the presence of all his people.
17 In the courts of the house of the Lord ■
in the midst of you, O Jerusalem. Alleluia.

A BIBLE READING

LIFE AS DISCIPLES OF CHRIST

Monday	*1 John 3: 10-16*
Tuesday	*2 John 1-6*
Wednesday	*Mark 16: 9-18*

Thursday	*Genesis 30: 25-43*
Friday	*Genesis 46: 28 - 47: 6*
Saturday	*Mark 6: 30-34*

or

Jesus himself stood among them and said to them, 'Peace be with you.' They were startled and terrified, and thought that they were seeing a ghost. He said to them, 'Why are you frightened, and why do doubts arise in your hearts? Look at my hands and my feet; see that it is I myself. Touch me and see; for a ghost does not have flesh and bones as you see that I have.' And when he had said this, he showed them his hands and his feet. While in their joy they were disbelieving and still wondering, he said to them,'Have you anything here to eat?' They gave him a piece of broiled fish, and he took it and ate in their presence.

Then he said to them, 'These are my words that I spoke to you while I was still with you – that everything written about me in the law of Moses, the prophets, and the psalms must be fulfilled.' Then he opened their minds to understand the scriptures, and he said to them, 'Thus it is written, that the Messiah is to suffer and to rise from the dead on the third day, and that repentance and forgiveness of sins is to be proclaimed in his name to all nations, beginning from Jerusalem. You are witnesses of these things.'

Luke 24: 36b-48

A CANTICLE

BENEDICITE

The Song of the Three 35-51

1 Bless the Lord all created things ▪
sing his praise and exalt him for ever.

2 Bless the Lord you heavens ▪
sing his praise and exalt him for ever.
3 Bless the Lord you angels of the Lord ▪
bless the Lord all you his hosts.
4 Bless the Lord you waters above the heavens ▪
sing his praise and exalt him for ever.
5 Bless the Lord sun and moon ▪
bless the Lord you stars of heaven.
6 Bless the Lord all rain and dew ▪
sing his praise and exalt him for ever.
7 Bless the Lord all winds that blow ▪
bless the Lord you fire and heat.
8 Bless the Lord scorching wind and bitter cold ▪
sing his praise and exalt him for ever.
9 Bless the Lord dews and falling snows ▪
bless the Lord you nights and days.
10 Bless the Lord light and darkness ▪
sing his praise and exalt him for ever.
11 Bless the Lord frost and cold ▪
bless the Lord you ice and snow.
12 Bless the Lord lightnings and clouds ▪
sing his praise and exalt him for ever.

Prayer

INTERCESSIONS AND THANKSGIVINGS

Pray that by showing greater love for one another people will know that Christians are disciples of Jesus. Pray that the Church may be more effective in its witness to Christ's victory over destructive forces in the world.
Give thanks for being able to worship freely and read and meditate on God's Word. Give thanks for all relationships in which we have known caring love.

Almighty Father,
who in your great mercy gladdened the disciples
with the sight of the risen Lord:
Give us such knowledge of his presence with us,
that we may be strengthened
and sustained by his risen life
and serve you continually in righteousness and truth;
through Jesus Christ our Lord. Amen.

or one of these prayers

Risen Christ,
you filled your disciples with boldness and fresh hope:
Strengthen us to proclaim your risen life
and fill us with your peace,
to the glory of God the Father. Amen.

Alternative Collects

God of mystery,
in a human body you showed your disciples
the marks of the crucified and living One.
Challenge us to respond to Christ
in the bodies of all who suffer,
so that the wounds which bring us healing
may be for the peace and salvation of all.
We ask this through Jesus Christ
who in glorious and undying life is one
with you and the Holy Spirit, now and for ever.

Celebrating the Christian Year

AN ENDING

Praise to you, Lord Jesus.
Dying, you destroyed our death,
rising you restored our life.
Lord Jesus, come in glory.

The Fourth Week of Easter

Preparation

A SENTENCE OF SCRIPTURE

In your unfailing love you will lead the people you have redeemed. In your strength you will guide them to your holy dwelling.

Exodus 15: 13 (TNIV)

A PRAYER OF PENITENCE

Almighty and most merciful Father;
we have erred and strayed from thy ways
like lost sheep.
We have followed too much the devices
and desires of our own hearts.
We have offended against thy holy laws.
We have left undone those things
which we ought to have done;
and we have done those things
which we ought not to have done;
and there is no health in us.
But thou, O Lord, have mercy upon us,
miserable offenders. Spare thou them, O God,
that confess their faults.
Restore thou them that are penitent;
according to thy promises
declared unto mankind in Christ Jesus our Lord.
And grant, O most merciful Father, for his sake;
that we may hereafter live a godly, righteous, and sober life, to the glory of thy holy Name. Amen.

The Lord's my Shepherd, I'll not want,
he makes me down to lie
in pastures green, he leadeth me
the quiet waters by.

My soul he doth restore again
and me to walk doth make
within the paths of righteousness,
e'en for his own Name's sake.

Yea, though I walk in death's dark vale,
yet will I fear none ill;
for thou art with me, and thy rod
and staff me comfort still.

My table thou hast furnishèd
in presence of my foes;
my head thou dost with oil anoint,
and my cup overflows.

Goodness and mercy all my life
shall surely follow me;
and in God's house for evermore
my dwelling place shall be.

William Whittingham (1524-79)

The Word of God

PSALM 95: 1-7

The Lord is my shepherd;
therefore can I lack nothing. ▪
Alleluia.

1 O come, let us sing to the Lord; ▪
let us heartily rejoice in the rock of our salvation.
2 Let us come into his presence with thanksgiving ▪
and be glad in him with psalms.

3 For the Lord is a great God ▪
and a great king above all gods.
4 In his hand are the depths of the earth ▪
and the heights of the mountains are his also.
5 The sea is his, for he made it, ▪
and his hands have moulded the dry land.
6 Come, let us worship and bow down ▪
and kneel before the Lord our Maker.
7 For he is our God; ▪
we are the people of his pasture
and the sheep of his hand.

A BIBLE READING

THE GOOD SHEPHERD

Monday	*1 Peter 5: 1-5*
Tuesday	*Revelation 7: 13-17*
Wednesday	*Mark 14: 26-31*

PROPHETIC VISIONS

Thursday	*Amos 8: 1-7*
Friday	*Amos 8: 11-13*
Saturday	*Amos 9: 7-15*

or

Jesus said, 'I am the good shepherd. The good shepherd lays down his life for the sheep. The hired hand, who is not the shepherd and does not own the sheep, sees the wolf coming and leaves the sheep and runs away – and the wolf snatches them and scatters them. The hired hand runs away because a hired hand does not care for the sheep. I am the good shepherd. I know my own and my own know me, just as the Father knows me and I know the Father. And I lay down my life for the sheep. I have other sheep that do not belong to this fold. I must bring them also, and they will listen to my voice. So there will be one flock, one shepherd. For this reason the Father loves me, because I lay down my life in order to take it up again. No one takes it from me, but I lay it down of my own accord. I have power to lay it down, and I have power to take it up again. I have received this command from my Father.'

John 10: 11-18

A CANTICLE

THE SONG OF ISAIAH

Isaiah 12: 2-6

1 Surely God is my salvation; ▪
I will trust, and will not be afraid :
2 for the Lord God is my strength and my might; ▪
he has become my salvation.
3 With joy you will draw water
from the wells of salvation ▪
And you will say in that day:
Give thanks to the Lord, call on his name;
4 Make known his deeds among the nations: ▪
proclaim that his name is exalted.
5 Sing praises to the Lord,
for he has done gloriously ▪
let this be known in all the earth.
6 Shout aloud and sing for joy, O royal Zion, ▪
for great in your midst is the Holy One of Israel.

Prayer

INTERCESSIONS AND THANKSGIVINGS

Pray for greater urgency in the search for unity in the worldwide church of Jesus Christ for becoming one flock with one Lord. Pray that all called to pastor the flock of Christ in the dangers of the world today especially in places where professing Christian faith lays a person in personal danger. Give thanks for the difference knowing Christ makes to life itself. Give thanks for all who venture into dangerous places in the service of humanity and the lost sheep of Christ's flock.

THE COLLECT OF EASTER 4

Almighty God,
whose Son Jesus Christ is the resurrection and the life:
Raise us, who trust in him,
from the death of sin to the life of righteousness,
that we may seek those things which are above,
where he reigns with you and the Holy Spirit,
one God, now and for ever. Amen.

or one of these prayers
Risen Christ,
faithful shepherd of your Father's sheep:
teach us to hear your voice
and to follow your command,
that all your people may be gathered into one flock,
to the glory of God the Father. Amen.

Alternative Collects

Good Shepherd of the sheep,
by whom the lost are sought
and guided into the fold:
Feed us and we shall be satisfied.
Heal us and we shall be whole.
Lead us where we may be with you,
with the Father and the Holy Spirit. Amen.

Prayer Book of New Zealand

THE LORD'S PRAYER

AN ENDING

Lord Jesus,
make us a people
whose song is alleluia,
whose sign is peace
and whose name is love
and you are all in all.

The Fifth Week of Easter

Preparation

A SENTENCE OF SCRIPTURE

I am the vine, you are the branches. If you remain in me and I in you , you will bear much fruit; apart from me you can do nothing.

John 15: 5 (TNIV)

A PRAYER OF PENITENCE

Most merciful Lord,
we have sinned and have not produced in our lives
the fruit you look for.
You have showered us with blessings
but we have turned our backs.
You have called us but we have stopped our ears
and done was right in our own eyes.
We know it is in your very nature to forgive
and so we ask you to break down the barriers
we have built,
to turn again and make us your own children.
Help us to be what you want.
Give us new lives with you and with our neighbours
against whom we have also sinned.
Father, we forgive those who sin against us,
so according to your promise we ask forgiveness
in the name of Jesus our redeemer. Amen.

HYMN

Abide among us with thy grace,
Lord Jesus, evermore,
nor let us e'er to sin give place,
nor grieve him we adore.

Abide among us with thy word,
Redeemer, whom we love;
thy help and mercy here afford,
and life with thee above.

Abide among us with thy ray,
O Light that lightenest all;
and let thy truth preserve our way,
nor suffer us to fall.

Abide with us to bless us still,
O bounteous Lord of peace;
with grace and power our spirits fill,
Our faith and love increase.

Abide with us in faithful love,
our God and Saviour be,
thy help at need O let us prove,
and keep us true to thee.

Joshua Stegman (1663-1713)

The Word of God

PSALM 80: 9-12, 15-16, 18-20

My beloved had a vineyard ▪
on a very fertile hill. Alleluia.

9 You brought a vine out of Egypt; ▪
you drove out the nations and planted it.
10 You made room around it, ▪
and when it had taken root, it filled the land.
11 The hills were covered with its shadow ▪
and the cedars of God by its boughs.
12 It stretched out its branches to the Sea ▪
and its tendrils to the River.
15 Turn again, O God of hosts, ▪
look down from heaven and behold;

16 Cherish this vine
which your right hand has planted, ▪
and the branch that you made
so strong for yourself.
18 Let your hand be upon the man
at your right hand, ▪
the son of man you made so strong for yourself.
19 And so will we not go back from you; ▪
give us life, and we shall call upon your name.
20 Turn us again, O God; ▪
show the light of your countenance,
and we shall be saved.

A BIBLE READING

I AM THE VINE

Monday *Isaiah 5: 1-7*
Tuesday *James 3: 17-18*
Wednesday *John 14: 18-31*

GOOD NEWS FOR ALL

Thursday *Isaiah 49: 5-6*
Friday *Isaiah 42: 5-9*
Saturday *Mark 10: 42-45*
or

Jesus said to his disciples, 'I am the true vine, and my Father is the vinegrower. He removes every branch in me that bears no fruit. Every branch that bears fruit he prunes to make it bear more fruit. You have already been cleansed by the word that I have spoken to you. Abide in me as I abide in you. Just as the branch cannot bear fruit by itself unless it abides in the vine, neither can you unless you abide in me. I am the vine, you are the branches. Those who abide in me and I in them bear much fruit, because apart from me you can do nothing. Whoever does not abide in me is thrown away like a branch and withers; such branches are gathered, thrown into the fire, and burned. If you abide in me, and my words abide in you, ask for whatever you wish, and it will be done for you. My Father is glorified by this, that you bear much fruit and become my disciples.'

John 15: 1-8

A CANTICLE

GLORY AND HONOUR

Revelation 4: 11 and 5:9, 10, 13b

1 Glory and honour and power ▪
are yours by right O Lord our God.
2 For your created all things ▪
and by your will they have their being.
3 Glory and honour and power ▪
are yours by right O Lamb for us slain;
4 For by your blood you ransomed us for God ▪
from every race and language
from every people and nation.
5 To make us a kingdom of priests ▪
to stand and serve before our God.
6 To him who sits on the throne and to the Lamb ▪
be praise and honour, glory and might
for ever and ever. Amen.

Prayer

INTERCESSIONS AND THANKSGIVINGS

Pray that the Church and all its members may bear fruit in mission and service, revealing the fruits of the Spirit in its life. Pray for all who mourn, for those are seriously ill and for all who have lost hope; that as they abide in Jesus they *may find peace and comfort. Give thanks that through baptism we have been grafted into the Vine which is Christ. Give thanks for all help to others to find new life and hope in the Lord Jesus and minister to those who have lost loved ones especially in tragic circumstances.*

THE COLLECT OF EASTER 5

Lord of all life and power,
who through the mighty resurrection of your Son
overcame the old order of sin and death
to make all things new in him:
Grant that we, being dead to sin
and alive to you in Jesus Christ,
may reign with him in glory;
to whom with you and the Holy Spirit
be praise and honour, glory and might,
now and in all eternity. Amen.

or one of these prayers
Eternal Father,
through the resurrection of your Son
help us to face the future
with courage and assurance,
secure in the knowledge
that nothing in death or life can ever separate us
from your love in Jesus Christ. Amen.

Risen Christ,
your wounds declare your love for the world
and the wonder of your risen life:
Give us compassion and courage
to risk ourselves for those we serve,
to the glory of God the Father. Amen.

Alternative Collects

THE LORD'S PRAYER

AN ENDING

Save us, Lord, while waking
and guard us while sleeping;
that awake we may watch with Christ,
and when we sleep rest in his peace. Amen.

The Sixth Week of Easter

Preparation

A SENTENCE OF SCRIPTURE

Jesus said: Anyone who loves me will obey my teaching. My Father will love them, and we will come to them and make our home with them.

John 14: 23 (TNIV)

A PRAYER OF PENITENCE

Heavenly Father,
we have sinned against you and against our neighbour
in thought and word and deed,
through negligence, through weakness,
through our own deliberate fault;
by what we have done
and by what we have failed to do.
We are truly sorry and repent of all our sins.
For the sake of your Son Jesus Christ who died for us,
forgive us all that is past;
and grant that we may serve you in newness of life
to the glory of your name. Amen.

HYMN

O Jesus, I have promised
to serve thee to the end;
be thou for ever near me,
my master and my friend.
I shall not fear the battle
if thou art by my side,
nor wander from the pathway,
if thou wilt be my guide.

O let me hear thee speaking
in accents clear and still,
above the storms of passion,
the murmurs of self-will.
O speak to reassure me,
to hasten or control:
O speak, and make me listen,
thou guardian of my soul.

O Jesus, thou hast promised
to all who follow thee,
that where thou art in glory,
there shall thy servant be;
and, Jesus, I have promised
to serve thee to the end;
O give me grace to follow
my master and my friend.

O let me see thy foot-marks,
and in them plant mine own;
my hope to follow duly
is in thy strength alone.
O guide me, call me, draw me,
uphold me to the end;
and then in heaven receive me,
my saviour and my friend.

John E Bode (1816-74)

The Word of God

PSALM 119: 97-104

Lead me in the path of your commandments. ▪
Alleluia.

97 Lord, how I love your law! ▪
All the day long it is my study.

98 Your commandments have made me wiser
than my enemies, ▪
for they are ever with me.
99 I have more understanding than all my teachers, ▪
for your testimonies are my meditation.
100 I am wiser than the aged, ▪
because I keep your commandments.
101 I restrain my feet from every evil way, ▪
that I may keep your word.
102 I have not turned aside from your judgments, ▪
for you have been my teacher.
103 How sweet are your words on my tongue! ▪
They are sweeter than honey to my mouth.
104 Through your commandments
I get understanding; ▪
therefore I hate all lying ways.

A BIBLE READING

KEEP MY COMMANDMENTS

Monday *Deuteronomy 7: 1-11*
Tuesday *Deuteronomy 11: 1-17*
Wednesday *Deuteronomy 11: 18-21*
or

Jesus said to his disciples: 'As the Father has loved me, so I have loved you; abide in my love. If you keep my commandments, you will abide in my love, just as I have kept my Father's commandments and abide in his love. I have said these things to you so that my joy may be in you, and that your joy may be complete. This is my commandment, that you love one another as I have loved you. No one has greater love than this, to lay down one's life for one's friends. You are my friends if you do what I command you. I do not call you servants any longer, because the servant does not know what the master is doing; but I have called you friends, because I have made known to you everything that I have heard from my Father. You did not choose me but I chose you. And I appointed you to go and bear fruit, fruit that will last, so that the Father will give you whatever you ask him in my name. I am giving you these commands so that you may love one another.'

John 15: 9-17

A CANTICLE

NUNC DIMITTIS

Luke 2: 29-32

1 Now, Lord, you let your servant go in peace; ▪
your word has been fulfilled.

2 My own eyes have seen the salvation ▪
which you have prepared
in the sight of every people.

3 A light to reveal you to the nations, ▪
and the glory of your people Israel.

Prayer

INTERCESSIONS AND THANKSGIVINGS

Pray for grace and strength to keep the commandments of Jesus. Pray for at this time for all those whose work sets food on our tables and pray for all in need. Pray for the work of all agencies which seek to alleviate hunger and distress in the face of natural and man-made disasters.

Give thanks for insights granted to men and women which have enriched human life especially in the fields of agriculture and medicine. Give thanks for all dedicated service to the poor and weak.

God our redeemer,
you have delivered us from the power of darkness
and brought us into the kingdom of your Son:
Grant, that as by his death he has recalled us to life
so by his continual presence in us
he may raise us to eternal joy;
through Jesus Christ our Lord. Amen.

or one of these prayers

Holy God,
you feed us with earthly and with spiritual food.
Deathless, unalterable,
you have chosen us, sinful as we are,
to hear your word and to proclaim your truth.
Alleluia! Make us salt to the earth;
make us yeast in the loaf. Amen.

Prayer Book of New Zealand

Safeguard the unity of your people, O God,
so that we whom Jesus calls friends
may keep his commandment of love.
For as he laid down his life for us,
so he now holds it glorious fulness,
with you and the Holy Spirit,
now and for ever. Amen.

Celebrating the Christian Year

THE LORD'S PRAYER

Into your hands, O Lord, I commend my spirit;
for your have redeemed me, O Lord God of truth.
Keep me as the apple of your eye;
hide me under the shadow of your wings.
In righteousness shall I see you;
your presence will give me joy.

The Ascension Day

Preparation

A SENTENCE OF SCRIPTURE

Jesus said: Go therefore, and make disciples of all nations, ... and remember, I am with you always, to the end of the age.

Matthew 28: 20

A PRAYER OF PENITENCE

Call to mind your sins of commission and omission, and bow before the ascended Lord.

Have mercy on us, O God, the Almighty,
Jesus Christ, Son of the living God;
Eternal Judge, have mercy.
Royal abundant Lord,
Great God, to whom we pray,
have mercy,
for it is your very nature to have mercy and to forgive;
thanks be to God.

HYMN

At the Name of Jesus
every knee shall bow,
every tongue confess him
King of glory now;
'tis the Father's pleasure
we should call him Lord,
who from the beginning
was the mighty Word.

Mighty and mysterious
in the highest height,
God from everlasting,
very Light of Light;
in the Father's bosom
with the Spirit blest,
love, in Love eternal,
rest in perfect rest.

Name him, brothers, name him,
with love as strong as death,
but with awe and wonder,
and with bated breath;
he is God the Saviour,
he is Christ the Lord,
ever to be worshipped,
trusted and adored.

Caroline Maria Noel (1817-77)

The Word of God

PSALM 8

The Lord is king, the Lord has put on his glory, ▪
Alleluia.

1 O Lord our governor, ▪
how glorious is your name in all the world!
2 Your majesty above the heavens is praised ▪
out of the mouths of babes at the breast.
3 You have founded a stronghold against your foes, ▪
that you might still the enemy and the avenger.
4 When I consider your heavens,
the work of your fingers, ▪
the moon and the stars that you have ordained,

5 What is man, that you should be mindful of him; ▪
the son of man, that you should seek him out?
6 You have made him little lower than the angels ▪
and crown him with glory and honour.
7 You have given him dominion
over the works of your hands ▪
and put all things under his feet,
8 All sheep and oxen,
even the wild beasts of the field, ▪
the birds of the air, the fish of the sea
and whatsoever moves in the paths of the sea.
9 O Lord our governor, ▪
how glorious is your name in all the world!

A BIBLE READING

In the first book, Theophilus, I wrote about all that Jesus did and taught from the beginning until the day when he was taken up to heaven, after giving instructions through the Holy Spirit to the apostles whom he had chosen. After his suffering he presented himself alive to them by many convincing proofs, appearing to them during forty days and speaking about the kingdom of God. While staying with them, he ordered them not to leave Jerusalem, but to wait there for the promise of the Father. 'This,' he said, 'is what you have heard from me; for John baptized with water, but you will be baptized with the Holy Spirit not many days from now.' So when Jesus and his disciples had come together, they asked him, 'Lord, is this the time when you will restore the kingdom to Israel?' He replied, 'It is not for you to know the times or periods that the Father has set by his own authority. But you will receive power when the Holy Spirit has come upon you; and you will be my witnesses in Jerusalem, in all Judea and Samaria, and to the ends of the earth.'

When he had said this, as they were watching, he was lifted up, and a cloud took him out of their sight. While he was going and they were gazing up toward heaven, suddenly two men in white robes stood by them. They said, 'Men of Galilee, why do you stand looking up toward heaven? This Jesus, who has been taken up from you into heaven, will come in the same way as you saw him go into heaven.'

Acts 1: 1-11

A CANTICLE

TE DEUM Part 1

1 We praise you, O God ▪
we acclaim you as the Lord;
2 All creation worships you ▪
the Father everlasting.
3 To you all angels, all the powers of heaven ▪
the cherubim and seraphim, sing in endless praise,
4 Holy, holy, holy Lord, God of power and might ▪
heaven and earth are full of your glory.
5 The glorious company of apostles praise you ▪
the noble fellowship of prophets praise you.
6 The white-robed army of martyrs praise you ▪
throughout the world,
the holy Church acclaims you.
7 Father, of majesty unbounded ▪
your true and only Son, worthy of all praise,
the Holy Spirit, advocate and guide.

Prayer

INTERCESSIONS AND THANKSGIVINGS

Pray for the nations of the world and their leaders, for peace and the reconciliation of all where differences divide men and women.

Give thanks for the apostolic gospel committed to the Church, for all works of compassion and for every service that proclaims God's love.

THE COLLECT OF THE DAY

Grant, we pray, Almighty God.
that as we believe your only-begotten Son
our Lord Jesus Christ
to have ascended into the heavens;
So we in heart and mind may also ascend
and with him continually dwell;
who is alive and reigns with you and the Holy Spirit,
one God, now and for ever. Amen.

or one of these prayers:

Eternal God,
set our hearts on Christ,
our risen and ascended Lord,
and clothe us with power from on high,
that Christ may continue to work
through the witness and worship of your people
until you bring that work to fulness
at his return in glory.
We ask this in the name of Jesus,
who is one with you and the Holy Spirit,
now and for ever. Amen.

Celebrating the Christian Year altd

Jesus Christ,
you left your disciples
only that you might send the Holy Spirit.
Grant us the Spirit of truth
to convince the world
that you are risen from the dead
and that to you all knees shall bow,
to the glory of God the Father. Amen.

THE LORD'S PRAYER

AN ENDING

Christ has opened the gate of glory;
Christ prays for us at the right hand of the Father.
Christ descended to lift us up to be with him.
Alleluia!

Days between the Ascension Day and Pentecost

Preparation

A SENTENCE OF SCRIPTURE

Go and make disciples of all nations, says the Lord; I am with you always, to the end of the age.

Matthew 28: 19, 20

A PRAYER OF PENITENCE

God our Father,
you exalted your Son to sit at your right hand.
Lord, have mercy.

Lord Jesus, you are the way, the truth and the life.
Christ, have mercy.

Holy Spirit, Counsellor,
you are sent to be with us for ever.
Lord, have mercy.

HYMN

Crown him with many crowns,
the Lamb upon his throne.
Hark! how the heavenly anthem drowns
all music but its own:
awake, my soul, and sing
of him who died for thee,
and hail him as thy matchless King
through all eternity.

Crown him the Lord of love.
Behold his hands and side,
those wounds, yet visible above,
in beauty glorified:

No angel in the sky
can fully bear that sight,
but downward bends his wondering eye
at mysteries so bright.

Crown him the Lord of Life
who triumphed o'er the grave,
and rose victorious in the strife,
for those he came to save:
his glories now we sing,
who died and rose on high,
who died eternal life to bring,
and lives that death may die.

Crown him the Lord of years,
the Potentate of time,
creator of the rolling spheres,
ineffably sublime:
All hail, Redeemer, hail!
for thou hast died for me;
thy praise shall never, never fail
throughout eternity.

Matthew Bridges (1800-94)
and Geoffrey Thring (1823-1903)

The Word of God

PSALM 47

As long as I have any being
I will sing praises to my God. ▪
Alleluia.

1 Clap your hands together, all you peoples; ▪
O sing to God with shouts of joy.
2 For the Lord Most High is to be feared; ▪
he is the great King over all the earth.

3 He subdued the peoples under us ▪
and the nations under our feet.
4 He has chosen our heritage for us, ▪
the pride of Jacob, whom he loves.
5 God has gone up with a merry noise, ▪
the Lord with the sound of the trumpet.
6 O sing praises to God, sing praises; ▪
sing praises to our King, sing praises.
7 For God is the King of all the earth; ▪
sing praises with all your skill.
8 God reigns over the nations; ▪
God has taken his seat upon his holy throne.
9 The nobles of the peoples are gathered together ▪
with the people of the God of Abraham.
10 For the powers of the earth belong to God ▪
and he is very highly exalted.

A BIBLE READING

Friday after the Ascension	*Revelation 1: 9-18*
Saturday after the Ascension	*John 16: 4-11*
Monday	*Philippians 1: 3-11*
Tuesday	*Titus 1: 1-9*
Wednesday	*John 16: 16-24*
Thursday	*1 Corinthians 15: 42b-49*
Friday	*1 Corinthians 15: 50-57*
Saturday	*John 7: 37-39*

or

Jesus continued in prayer to his Father, saying, 'I have made your name known to those whom you gave me from the world. They were yours, and you gave them to me, and they have kept your word. Now they know that everything you have given me is from you; for the words that you gave to me I have given to them, and they have received them and know in truth that I came from you; and they have believed that you sent me. I am asking on their behalf; I am not asking on behalf of the world, but on behalf of those whom you gave me, because they are yours. All mine are yours, and yours are mine; and I have been glorified in them. And now I am no longer in the world, but they are in the world, and I am coming to you. Holy Father, protect them in your name that you have given me, so that they may be one, as we are one. While I was with them, I protected them in your name that you have given me. I guarded them, and not one of them was lost except the one destined to be lost, so that the scripture might be fulfilled. But now I am coming to you, and I speak these things in the world so that they may have my joy made complete in themselves. I have given them your word, and the world has hated them because they do not belong to the world, just as I do not belong to the world. I am not asking you to take them out of the world, but I ask you to protect them from the evil one. They do not belong to the world, just as I do not belong to the world. Sanctify them in the truth; your word is truth. As you have sent me into the world, so I have sent them into the world. And for their sakes I sanctify myself, so that they also may be sanctified in truth.'

John 17: 9-19

A SONG OF CHRIST'S GLORY

Philippians 2: 5-11

1 Christ Jesus was in the form of God; ▪
but he did not cling to equality with God.
2 He emptied himself, taking the form of a servant ▪
and was born in our human likeness.
3 And being found in human form
he humbled himself ▪
and became obedient unto death
even death on a cross.
4 Therefore God has highly exalted him: ▪
and bestowed on him the name above every name.
5 That at the name of Jesus every knee should bow: ▪
in heaven and on earth and under the earth.
6 And every tongue confess
that Jesus Christ is Lord: ▪
to the glory of God the Father.

Prayer

INTERCESSIONS AND THANKSGIVINGS

Pray in these nine days for the renewal of the church by the power of the Holy Spirit; for that unity of the church for which Christ prayed and by the means he shall choose; for renewed obedience to the Great Commission to preach the Gospel to all the world.

Give thanks for the heritage we have received from the times of the apostles, for the mission in which God has called us to share, for the will to unity, and its fruit in common action.

O God the King of Glory,
you have exalted your only Son Jesus Christ
with great triumph to your kingdom in heaven:
Mercifully give us faith to know
that, as he promised,
he abides with us on earth to the end of time;
who is alive and reigns with you and the Holy Spirit,
one God, now and for ever. Amen.

or these prayers:
Risen ascended Lord,
as we rejoice at your triumph,
fill your church on earth with power and compassion,
that all who are estranged by sin
may find forgiveness and know your peace,
to the glory of God the Father. Amen.

Alternative Collects

Gracious and glorious God,
you have chosen us as your own,
and by the powerful name of Christ
you protect us from evil.
By your Spirit transform us and your beloved world,
that we may find our joy in your Son,
Jesus Christ, our Saviour and Lord,
whom with you and the Holy Spirit
we worship and praise,
one God, now and for ever. Amen.

Lutheran Renewing Worship

AN ENDING

To God, who by the power at work within us,
is able to do far more abundantly
than all we ask or think,
to him be glory in the church and in Christ Jesus
to all generations for ever and ever. Amen.

Ephesians 3: 20

The Day of Pentecost

Preparation

A SENTENCE OF SCRIPTURE

When the day of Pentecost had come ... All of them were filled with the Holy Spirit. and began to speak in other languages, as the Spirit gave them ability.

Acts 2: 1, 4

A PRAYER OF PENITENCE

Holy God,
we have sinned against your Spirit
and against one another.
We pray for your goodness and healing.
The Holy Spirit reveals to us our offences.
The good we want to do, we often fail to do.
The evil we do not want, we find ourselves doing.
Deliver us, good Lord,
save us from shame
and guide us in your way;
for the sake of Jesus Christ our Lord. Amen.

HYMN

O thou who camest from above
the pure celestial fire to impart,
kindle a flame of sacred love
on the mean altar of my heart.

There let it for thy glory burn
with ever-bright, undying blaze,
and trembling to its source return
in humble prayer, and fervent praise.

Jesus, confirm my heart's desire
to work, and speak, and think for thee;
still let me guard the holy fire,
and still stir up thy gift in me.

Still let me prove thy perfect will,
my act of faith and love repeat;
till death thy endless mercies seal,
and make the sacrifice complete.

Charles Wesley (1707-88)

The Word of God

PSALM 138

Send your Holy Spirit and clothe us
with power from on high. ■
Alleluia.

1 I will give thanks to you, O Lord,
with my whole heart; ■
before the gods will I sing praise to you.
2 I will bow down towards your holy temple
and praise your name,
because of your love and faithfulness; ■
for you have glorified your name
and your word above all things.
3 In the day that I called to you, you answered me; ■
you put new strength in my soul.
4 All the kings of the earth shall praise you, O Lord, ■
for they have heard the words of your mouth.
5 They shall sing of the ways of the Lord, ■
that great is the glory of the Lord.
6 Though the Lord be high,
he watches over the lowly; ■
as for the proud, he regards them from afar.

7 Though I walk in the midst of trouble,
you will preserve me; ▪
you will stretch forth your hand
against the fury of my enemies;
your right hand will save me.
8 The Lord shall make good his purpose for me; ▪
your loving-kindness, O Lord, endures for ever;
for sake not the work of your hands.

A BIBLE READING

Jesus said, 'When the Advocate comes, whom I will send to you from the Father, the Spirit of truth who comes from the Father, he will testify on my behalf. You also are to testify because you have been with me from the beginning. I did not say these things to you from the beginning, because I was with you. But now I am going to him who sent me; yet none of you asks me, "Where are you going?" But because I have said these things to you, sorrow has filled your hearts. Nevertheless I tell you the truth: it is to your advantage that I go away, for if I do not go away, the Advocate will not come to you; but if I go, I will send him to you. And when he comes, he will prove the world wrong about sin and righteousness and judgment: about sin, because they do not believe in me; about righteousness, because I am going to the Father and you will see me no longer; about judgment, because the ruler of this world has been condemned. I still have many things to say to you, but you cannot bear them now.

When the Spirit of truth comes, he will guide you into all the truth; for he will not speak on his own, but will speak whatever he hears, and he will declare to you the things that are to come. He will glorify me, because he will take what is mine and declare it to you. All that the Father has is mine. For this reason I said that he will take what is mine and declare it to you.'

John 15: 26-27; 16: 4b-15

A CANTICLE

GREAT AND WONDERFUL

Revelation 15: 3,4 and 7: 10,12

1 Great and wonderful are your deeds Lord God,
the Almighty, ▪
just and true are your ways, O King of the nations.
2 Who shall not revere
and praise your name, O Lord ▪
for you alone are holy.
3 All nations shall come
and worship in your presence ▪
for your just dealings have been revealed.
4 To him who sits on the throne, and to the Lamb ▪
be praise and honour, glory and might,
for ever and ever. Amen.

Prayer

INTERCESSIONS AND THANKSGIVINGS

Pray for the renewal and unity of the church worldwide; for peace among all those who believe in God's providence and his work in people of different races and creeds; that people may walk in love, joy and peace.
Give thanks for the Spirit whose working gives life to the church and who transforms human lives.

THE COLLECT OF PENTECOST

Almighty God,
who on the day of Pentecost
sent your Holy Spirit to the apostles
with the wind from heaven and in tongues of flame,
filling them with joy
and boldness to preach the gospel:
By the power of the same Spirit
strengthen us to witness to your truth
and to draw everyone to the fire of your love;
through Jesus Christ our Lord. Amen.

or one of these prayers:

God of power,
may the boldness of your Spirit transform us,
the gentleness of your Spirit lead us,
and may the gifts of your Spirit equip us to serve
and worship you now and always;
through Jesus Christ our Lord. Amen.

Prayer Book of New Zealand

Holy Spirit, sent by the Father,
ignite in us your holy fire:
Strengthen your children with the gift of faith,
revive your church with the breath of love,
and renew the face of the earth;
through Jesus Christ our Lord. Amen.

Alternative Collects

THE LORD'S PRAYER

AN ENDING

The Spirit of truth lead us into all truth,
give us grace to confess that Jesus is Lord
and to proclaim the word and works of God. Amen.

Acknowledgements

Texts are reproduced with the permission of the copyright owners from:

The Book of Common Prayer of the Church of Ireland (Revision of 2004) © 2004 Representative Church Body, Church of Ireland House, Dublin 6.

Bible passages are from the *New Revised Standard Version*, Anglicized edition.© 1989, 1995 by the Division of Christian Education of the National Council of Churches of Christ in the USA, and are used by permission. All rights reserved..

Sentences indicated by TNIV are from *Today's New International Version* (TNIV) © 2002 by the International Bible Society. Used by permission of Hodder and Stoughton Publishers. All rights reserved.

Psalms are from the Psalter in *Common Worship: Services and Prayers for the Church of England* © 2000 by Archbishops' Council.

Several of the prayers alternative to the collect are also from *Common Worship: Alternative Collects* © 2004 by Archbishops' Council.

The canticles, Te Deum and *Nunc Dimittis* are © 1988 English Language Liturgical Consultation (ELLC).

A New Zealand Prayer Book © 1988 The Church of the Province of New Zealand Aot.

Lutheran Renewal Worship © 2004 Fortress Press.

Revised Common Lectionary Prayers ©2002 Consultation on Common Texts.

Celebrating the Christian Year, Volume 2, compiled by Alan Griffiths, © 2005, published by Canterbury Press, Norwich.

Bible citations from *Revised Common Lectionary Daily Readings* ©Consultation on Common Texts. Used by permission.

Other texts are by the compiler. If, through inadvertence, copyright material has been used without permission or acknowledgement the publisher will be grateful to be informed and will make the necessary correction in a subsequent edition.